CARR CLIFTON
NEW YORK
IMAGES OF THE LANDSCAPE

PHOTOGRAPHY BY CARR CLIFTON

WESTCLIFFE PUBLISHERS, INC. ENGLEWOOD, COLORADO

CONTENTS

International Standard Book Number: ISBN: 0-942394-57-7
Library of Congress Catalogue Card Number: 87-051502
Copyright, Photographs and Text: Carr Clifton, 1988
Editor: John Fielder
Assistant Editors: Scott Lankford, Margaret Terrell Morse
Production Manager: Mary Jo Lawrence
Typographer: Dianne J. Borneman
Printer: Dai Nippon Printing Company, Ltd.,Tokyo, Japan
Publisher: Westcliffe Publishers, Inc.
2650 South Zuni Street
Englewood, Colorado 80110

Bibliography, John Burroughs' Quotations

All quotations excerpted from *John Burroughs' America*, ed. Farida A. Wiley. Reprinted by
permission of Devin-Adair Publishers, Greenwich, Connecticut; Copyright © 1951.

---

*First frontispiece: Early morning light on Heart Lake,
Adirondack Park and Preserve*

Second frontispiece: Cluster of lupine, Chautauqua County

*Third frontispiece: Freshly fallen leaves after snowstorm,
Shawangunk Mountains*

*Title page: Oak leaves and pine needles float upon North Lake,
Catskill Mountains Park and Preserve*

*Right: Pink lady's slipper adds a colorful accent to the
forest floor, Allegany State Park*

FOREWORD

The New York that Carr Clifton shows us once dwelled in every American's imagination. The art of the Hudson River School, the stories of James Fenimore Cooper and Washington Irving, the tales of Adirondack hunters and Catskill fishermen; these first gave Americans an image of nature other than a beast to be subdued. Nineteenth-century New York was the Empire State not only for the thrusting energy of its inhabitants, but also for the matchless grandeur of its land.

In the 20th century, the glitz of metropolis has elbowed aside this older sense of New York. Today, New York is New York City, the glittering modern Babylon, with all the pleasures and perils thereof. To fault New York City for this is unfair. It is the capital of the world, overflowing with energy and wonders. Yet there remains another New York, quiet, serene, but also full of wonders. Now, in this happy combination of Carr Clifton's evocative pictures and John Burroughs's felicitous words, we discover it again.

This is a New York of lakes, matchless lakes — Champlain and George, Oneida and Chautauqua, Ontario and Erie, the long-reaching Finger Lakes that the glaciers drove through central New York's rolling hills, the high mountain lakes of the Adirondacks, hundreds of blue jewels perfectly set in ancient metamorphic rock.

This is a New York of mountains — the Adirondacks and the Catskills, the Shawangunks and the Taconics. New York's mountains are old, shaped by time, full of wisdom. Wander among them and the long history of nature, of life, rushes up to meet you.

This is a New York of hills and highlands. Once they held so many farmers that New York was America's breadbasket, its leading wheat producer. Now, the farmers sadly dwindled, tree, bush and flower have reclaimed their domain and New York, yes New York, has become the most forested state in the country.

This is a New York of rivers, rivers of fame — the Hudson, North America's fjord; the Saint Lawrence with its thousand islands; the Susquehanna, gathering the waters that nourish the Chesapeake; the Allegheny, flowing southwestward to create the Ohio; the Delaware; the Mohawk; the Niagara, with America's greatest waterfall; the Genesee; the fabled white waters of the Adirondack's west slope; and the quick, flashing streams of the Catskills.

Add to this New York Long Island, 110 miles long, in size and character an island without a serious American rival. This New York is pine barrens and kettle ponds, spring-fed brown water streams that pour off glacial ridges into great bays, barrier beaches and a treasure of tidal wetlands.

For such riches to provide their unique tonic to the human spirit, they must be properly presented. First introductions matter. That task, of introduction, of appreciation, of celebration, Carr Clifton flawlessly accomplishes here. His deft, sure photographic vision gives all who love nature a magnificent new gift — New York.

In his preface, Carr Clifton speaks of his mounting exhilaration as his camera took him beyond the popular image of New York to discover its natural treasures. Yet what he has provided us is not so much a discovery as a return, a return to a major part of the American outdoor heritage, the New York our ancestors knew. We have neglected our New York heritage; too long we have been without the delight and inspiration our ancestors drew from it.

From this New York have come magnificent inspirations. It was New Yorkers who, in 1885, created the six-million-acre Adirondack forest preserve, by state constitutional enactment "forever wild," and gave conservation its first great triumph over rip, ruin and run thinking. Two years later, other New York outdoor enthusiasts formed the Boone and Crockett Club, dedicated to the principle that hunting should be a sport that respects wildlife, not a bloodletting that mindlessly massacres it. Prominent among that inspired band was a young New York patrician named Theodore Roosevelt. Twenty years later, as president, Roosevelt would draw on a New York-nurtured passion for nature to articulate an American conservation ethic that to this day both shapes and challenges our relationship to the American land.

Today in New York echoes of those years are heard again. The pulse of conservation action quickens every year. Abetted by public sentiment reawakening to New York's outdoor heritage, and bolstered by the irrefutable evidence of the economic costs of environmental mismanagement, progress is being made toward forging a new conservation consensus in New York. Great perils threaten this New York that Carr Clifton has recaptured for us — acid rain, toxic pollutions, misplaced hydro-development, thoughtless chop-chop land development. But great energies are being mobilized too, recognizing, as Clifton urges, not only the urgency of the time, but the unique natural treasures that New York possesses. Hopefully all who encounter the New York land in the future will bring to it the eye Carr Clifton has, so that we may recapture this seminal American heritage and make provision to insure that in another century New York will still be here to enrapture.

— ALBERT F. APPLETON
Co-founder, New York City Audubon Society

Red maple contrasts with white pine, Adirondack Park and Preserve

PREFACE

"The most precious things of life are near at hand, without money and without price. Each of you has the whole wealth of the universe at your very door. All that I ever had, and still have, may be yours by stretching forth your hand and taking it."

Thus wrote John Burroughs of his beloved New York State at a time when its natural beauties were as accessible to every man, woman and child as the air they breathed. Now, less than a century later, much of New York's natural landscape is blighted by man's industrial "progress," and "the wealth of the universe" may seem only a romantic abstraction. One wonders if Burroughs's happy assertion can still be true or if it is merely the antiquated optimism of a man who lived when America's most ample resource was her untrampled and wild places.

This selection of Carr Clifton's photographs, *New York, Images of the Landscape*, is a testament, a reminder that Burroughs's statement still holds for those whose patience, determination and faith enable them to see the delicate designs of nature so often obscured by the distractions of our hurried and bottled-up lives. Burroughs's writings and Clifton's photographs together invite us to look more closely and carefully at our world. They also challenge us to take a deeper look at ourselves, to discover ourselves within a landscape and to integrate our sense of being with a living earth in sidereal time. "Dignity and beauty and meaning are given to our lives when we see far enough and wide enough," wrote Burroughs, "when we see the forces that minister to us, and the natural order of which we form a part."

To see far and wide, and to know ourselves in the natural order can be painful. As Burroughs noted, "One's own landscape comes in time to be a sort of outlying part of [one]self . . .: cut those trees, and [one] bleeds; mar those hills, and [one] suffers." When the earth is subjected daily to violence, that violence is eventually recognized for what it is — violence to ourselves. It is only through such recognition and with the depth and conviction of that terrible knowledge that we can hope to preserve both our spiritual and biological integrity in this time of environmental devastation. To Burroughs, spirit is wed to matter, and God and nature are one. Reverence for and knowledge of the earth can engender an attitude that can heal both it and ourselves, an attitude, according to Burroughs, ". . . in which personal hopes, individual good, and the so-called 'other world' play little part . . . and the security of the future is in well-doing and well-being in the present . . . [an attitude] that opens our eyes to the wonders and beauty of the world and that makes us at home in this world."

We are home. Clifton's photographs are images of our home. Perhaps they remind us of a home we have abandoned, lost or forgotten, but nonetheless a home of which we are a part. To know our home we must go out into it or, with the help of these images, remember how we have done so in the past. With great love and patience Carr Clifton has framed these tender, living moments in the New York landscape. It is for the viewer now to step inside each frame.

— ELISA ADLER

Editor's Introduction

John Burroughs was born on a farm at the foot of the Catskill Mountains in 1837. His first book of nature essays, *Wake-Robin*, was published in 1871. By the time of his death in 1921, Burroughs had become the most popular and prolific American nature writer of his time. Over the course of his 50-year career, he published literally hundreds of articles and dozens of books. Some of his books were even used as textbooks in many American high schools beginning in 1888. Despite his nationwide fame, Burroughs preferred to spend most of his time living in and writing about his home state. His special love for the natural environment of New York State shines forth in the quotations selected to accompany this collection of photographic images.

— Scott Lankford
Program in Modern Thought and Literature
Stanford University

Atlantic sea scallop shells blanket Northwest Harbor's shores, Long Island

CARR CLIFTON

New York. For many of us the very name conjures images of concrete spires thrusting toward the sky, a beehive of world finance, media and fashion, the hum of factories. We imagine millions of commuters making their daily migrations; horns honking like geese in flight, or well-worn taxis worming their way through traffic. We think of the Statue of Liberty and the melting pot of people she inspires; hear the air traffic, trains and shipyards; and smell the aroma of international cuisine. That New York is a city that encompasses only a minute portion of the landmass of New York State. But there is another New York, a New York where water, forest and mountains dominate the landscape, a New York I discovered by accident on my hurried way to someplace else.

I was raised in the rural West, so I'm familiar with vast spaces and long distances. I have tramped mile after mile of the Sierra Nevada crest in search of the expansive picture, and my eyes have learned to bring the distant horizon into focus as I seek to preserve with photographic images the grandeur of wild places I love.

Because my eyes have been drawn 3,000 feet up a Yosemite wall or hundreds of miles across a shimmering desert to a sudden range of granite mountains, it's understandable that I have been distracted from the subtleties at my feet. The vastness of the western landscape inspires photographs that emphasize the magnificence of the great and the bold. In my photographs of the West, as in so much western photography, the landscape, the place itself dominates the frame.

The West, with its wealth of open spaces, has taught me something of wilderness and solitude. It has taught me how to think big, to look far and beyond myself. The East has shown me something different. Amid the relative calm of the eastern landscape, I have been able to look more closely, to find beauty and wildness in intimate spaces and near horizons. After six trips to New York and a solid 16 weeks of daily photographing, I am now able to describe in words my new way of seeing and framing the landscape. I learned to let time slow down. I drew my attention to the immediate. I paused.

Just months ago, I thought of New York as an obstacle to get through as quickly as possible. Bound for New England in search of the famous autumn colors, I had been driving 15-hour shifts every day for almost a week to get where I thought I was going. One morning near dawn, I was jittery from too much bad coffee and mesmerized by the white lines on the highway. Then, somewhere near Lake Placid, a loon called, and the mist rising from a steamy lake, golden with morning, woke me from my blind rushing. Something stopped me. I saw a frosty canoe part the glassy waters of a lake, reflecting flames of glowing leaves. I stopped, and in that stopping the world rushed in to fill me. I remained to photograph, and so began my discovery of New York, the state I had never intended to know.

In the Adirondacks I photographed for the first time deep within a hardwood forest. The lakes and ponds were the color of rich, dark tea from the tannic acid that leached from the surrounding woodlands. I looked down and saw brilliant red, orange and purple leaves suspended on those black waters. I looked deeper and longer and saw the now-bare trees reflected in patterns with the leaves.

Everything I saw was new to me: wet, brilliant and delicate. Compared to the massive, towering and vertical green forests of the West, the Adirondack mountain forest seemed an undulating carpet, an awesome mosaic of shifting color.

I photographed New York in all seasons. My first exploration was in fall, and I was intoxicated by color. When I returned in winter, it was the lack of color that struck me. I spent February in the same folds of the Adirondacks that I'd photographed just months before, but this time all was gray and accentuated by light and shadow. Without the distraction of brilliant color, I was able to concentrate on detail, pattern and form in a vast realm of snow.

(continued on next page)

Autumn leaves grace the Ardsley House, Catskill Mountains Park and Preserve

Winter is a time when many people stay indoors and contemplate the passing season through frosty windowpanes. Winter for me meant waxing up my skis, wrapping myself in wool, pile and Gore-Tex, and heading out to explore. I felt like a child on his first outing, giggling as I glided across frozen ponds and snow-dusted meadows. I followed meandering creeks hushed by a blanket of snow, and pushed deeper into a forest made silver by the bare limbs of eastern hardwoods. All was quiet but the sound of my skis and breathing, and the sound of trees popping as the sap within them froze in the bracing cold.

Spring in New York showed me the intensity of eastern green. Winter's gray had been overwhelmed by green; a sprawling canopy of leaves filtered the light reaching the forest floor and created a sweet hue of popsicle green. The rivers and brooks, which only weeks earlier had been muted and narrow, swelled and filled with rushing sound.

I explored the Hudson in spring. After driving hundreds of miles up and down both sides of its banks, I finally got a sense of the place and was able to find a vantage point where I could show the enormity of the river and surrounding highlands. That accomplished, I climbed down to the water's edge to pursue a more intimate landscape, to frame the small-scale compositions that intrigue me most.

By then it was evident to me that New York is one of the nation's most underrated states, at least in terms of natural landscape. Nevertheless, I was reluctant to venture toward Long Island. In fact, Long Island was the last place I wanted to go because it meant driving through the New York City area. Although I'm fine on windy peaks, I'm not high on skyscrapers and have been a proclaimed city-avoider for as long as I can remember. Since Long Island is so close to the city, I was sure it would be overcrowded, that I wouldn't be able to concentrate and that it would be impossible to get any acceptable photographs. So I hurried again. This time I traveled through the Bronx and across the 118-mile-long island to the easternmost tip at Montauk Point. There, to my surprise, I found spotless towns, fog-shrouded lighthouses and ospreys nesting along the coastal estuaries of looking-glass bays. I learned the beauty of manmade objects in a landscape. I saw old salt-sprayed dories filled with rainwater dotting the shell-covered beaches. I was reminded of how man and the land are linked by elements and time.

New York. The Finger Lakes, the Hudson, Lake Ontario, Lake Erie, the Saint Lawrence River, Niagara Falls, the Catskills, the Alleghenies, the Shawangunk Mountains; these names and others describe the character of New York. They describe a land of water, forest and mountains. I wonder if these names will describe the New York of the future.

The images on these pages represent my photographic discovery of New York and are a testament to the beauty I perceived there. But they mustn't be mistaken for a true representation of the state, for they are only images discovered in the places where I chose to linger.

Beyond the veneer of these flat photographic surfaces is a region threatened by acid rain. Missing from this collection are images of the dead and dying conifers that top the highest ridges of the northeastern mountain ranges. Missing also are photographs that show the uncanny blue of now-sterile lakes once teeming with aquatic life. I took no pictures of the loon chicks that starve to death each spring because the sterile lakes can't support the living organisms they feed upon, nor of the fingerlings that float to the surface of some uninhabitable waters.

Every photographer knows that time is of the essence, and that the same moment never comes twice. Unless the photographs on these pages are to become mere shadows of a place that was, we must learn now to look closely and deeply. We must recognize the urgency of our time and, knowing that our fate is linked with that of the water, mountains and trees, make environmental protection the priority of this and every decade.

— CARR CLIFTON

This book is dedicated in memory of my brother Cole McCoy Clifton.

Spring runoff feeds Taughannock Fall, Taughannock Falls State Park

COLOR

Not all of Earth's creatures are blessed with the ability to see color. Humans are fortunate — we discern varying hues in a world that other animals see as black and white. Color is the spice of sight, adding that last but most fascinating accent.

Abundant fall colors, Delaware County

Barn and freshly fallen snow near Lake Placid,
Adirondack Park and Preserve

Duckweed abounds in marsh, Iroquois National Wildlife Refuge

Overleaf: Irises greet spring's arrival with a colorful display,
Red House Lake, Allegany State Park

"
. . . the student and lover of nature has this advantage
over people who gad up and down the world seeking some
novelty or excitement: he has only to stay at home and see
the procession pass. . . .

Wet maple leaves on rock, Catskill Mountains Park and Preserve

Sunset shimmers across Oneida Lake, Oneida County

. . . The great globe swings around to him like a revolving showcase; the change of the seasons is like the passage of strange and new countries; . . .

Mountain winterberry covered in ice, Shawangunk Mountains

Mountain winterberry adorns maple trunk,
Shawangunk Mountains

. . . the zones of the earth, with all their beauties and
marvels, pass one's door and linger long in the passing."

Captured enemy cannons, West Point Military Academy

Old gas pump, Orient Point, Long Island

Overleaf: Fall-colored forest mirrors on Heart Lake,
Adirondack Park and Preserve

"To attempt to manufacture beauty is as vain as to
attempt to manufacture truth; and to give it to us in poems
or any form of art, without a lion of some sort, a lion
of truth or fitness or power, is to emasculate and
destroy its volition."

Vibrant ferns grace spring forest, Allegany State Park

Red maple and rock, Catskill Mountains Park and Preserve

"*All true beauty in nature or in art is like the iridescent hue of mother-of-pearl, . . .*

Wild geranium adds vibrant color to spring greenery,
Hudson Valley

Shelf fungus, Madison County

. . . which is intrinsic and necessary, being the result of the
arrangement of the particles. . . ."

Aluminum boats piled in formation, Allegany State Park

Abandoned house, Adirondack Park and Preserve

Overleaf: Brilliant colors carpet the forest understory,
Wyoming County

"
. . . beauty as a separate and distinct thing does not exist.
Neither can it be reached by any sorting or sifting or
clarifying process. . . .

Stately trees grace the Vanderbilt Mansion, Hudson Valley

Blanket of red maple leaves, Adirondack Park and Preserve

. . . It is an experience of the mind, and must be preceded
by the conditions, . . .

Multicolored fishing buoys, Village of Orient, Long Island

*Fall's vibrantly colored ferns and sugar maples,
Adirondack Park and Preserve*

*. . . just as light is an experience of the eye,
and sound of the ear.''*

FORM

Form is almost more a sense of touch than it is of sight. The eyes feel edges and shapes; they trace outlines and follow wanderings.

Maple sapling against pine trunk, Bear Mountain State Park

Overleaf: Rays of sun accentuate ridgelines around Lake Placid, Adirondack Park and Preserve

Sunrise on fog-shrouded pond, Adirondack Park and Preserve

Maple leaves and reflected maple tree in pond,
Adirondack Park and Preserve

"*The clouds are pearly and iridescent and seem the*
farthest possible remove from the condition of a storm —
the ghosts of clouds, the indwelling beauty freed
from all dross."

Ice-covered rocks, Pillar Point, Lake Ontario

Red maples and ferns, Adirondack Park and Preserve

"*The rocks are not so close akin to us as the soil; they are one more remove from us; but they lie back of all and are the final source of all.*"

Beech tree and balsam fir covered in fresh snowfall,
Adirondack Park and Preserve

Large-flowered trillium renews the forest floor, Finger Lakes

Overleaf: False hellebore overwhelms the forest floor,
Allegany State Park

"*Nature is always new in the spring, and lucky are we if
it finds us new also.*"

Long shadows enhance the winter forest, Shawangunk Mountains

Fall-colored maple highlights barren forest,
Adirondack Park and Preserve

"What a multitude of sins this unstinted charity of the
snow covers! How it flatters the ground! . . . It is like some
conjurer's trick. The very trees have turned to snow. . . .

Autumn colors settle on pond, Adirondack Mountains

Snow blankets the east branch of the Ausable River,
Adirondack Park and Preserve

. . . The smallest branch is like a cluster of great
white antlers. The eye is bewildered by the soft fleecy
labyrinth before it. . . . It is a new kind of foliage
wrought by the frost and the clouds, . . .

Drifted snow blankets country barn,
Adirondack Park and Preserve

Bare maple trees, Shawangunk Mountains

Overleaf: Abundant water lilies on pond, Adirondack Mountains

. . . and it obscures the sky and fills the vistas of the woods
nearly as much as the myriad leaves of summer."

Fern fiddleheads emerge from blackened waters,
near Verona Beach

Ice-frosted windowpane, Jefferson County

"*I know of nothing in vegetable nature that seems so
really to be born as the ferns. They emerge from the
ground rolled up, . . . and appear to need a maternal
tongue to lick them into shape. The sun plays the wet nurse
to them, and very soon they are out of that uncanny
covering . . .*"

Marble columns of the Vanderbilt Mansion, overlooking the Hudson River

The low sun of winter, Shawangunk Mountains

"*M*an can have but one interest in nature, namely, to see himself reflected or interpreted there, and we quickly neglect both poet and philosopher who fail to satisfy, in some measure, this feeling."

Bare limbs soften the winter hillside,
Catskill Mountains Park and Preserve

Cascading water of Chittenango Falls,
Chittenango Falls State Park

"*One's own landscape comes in time to be a sort of*
outlying part of himself; he has sowed himself broadcast
upon it, . . .

Abstract patterns on beaver pond, Harriman State Park

Fresh snowfall along Lake Clear outlet,
Adirondack Park and Preserve

. . . and it reflects his own moods and feelings; he is
sensitive to the verge of the horizon: cut those trees, and he
bleeds; mar those hills, and he suffers."

MOMENT

In these photographs, the image is dominated by the moment in time when the scene was discovered. A camera lens can capture a fraction of a second in time, or span an eternity. Moment can express an entire season, or that fleeting interlude between fall and winter.

Red maple in clearing mist, Adirondack Park and Preserve

*Overleaf: Golden glow of sunset over Lake Durant,
Adirondack Park and Preserve*

Beech tree in fog, Shawangunk Mountains

Winter ice chokes the Raquette River,
Adirondack Park and Preserve

"*The power to see straight is the rarest of gifts: to see no*
more and no less than is actually before you; . . .

Wind-blown trees along icy shore, Lake Ontario

Sunrise over Genesee River Gorge, Letchworth State Park

*. . . to be able to detach yourself and see the thing as it
actually is, uncolored or unmodified by your own
sentiments or prepossessions. . . .*

Montauk Point Lighthouse, Long Island

Mature oaks in snowstorm, Shawangunk Mountains

. . . *In short, to see with your reason as well as with your perceptions, that is to be an observer and to read the book of nature aright."*

Whiteface Mountain illuminates at sunset,
Adirondack Park and Preserve

Dock pilings at sunset, Northwest Harbor, Long Island

Overleaf: Trapps Ridge above beaver pond,
Shawangunk Mountains

. . . I find that each spring, each summer and fall and
winter of my life, has a hue and quality of its own, . . .

Family farm near the Saint Lawrence River, Jefferson County

Formation of leaves and foam on Marcy Brook,
Adirondack Mountains

*. . . given by some prevailing mood, a train of thought, an
event, an experience — a color or quality of which I am
quite unconscious at the time, being too near to it and too
completely enveloped by it. . . .*

Water lily and clouds reflected on pond, Niagara County

Hay rake and barn north of Saranac Lake,
Adirondack Park and Preserve

. . . But afterward some mood or circumstance, an odor, or
fragment of a tune, brings it back as by a flash. . . ."

Rays of sun reflect off built-up ice,
Lake Ontario near Cape Vincent

Rock slabs overlook Lake Placid, Adirondack Park and Preserve

"*Rocks do not recommend the land to the tiller of the soil,*
but they recommend it to those who reap a harvest of
another sort — the artist, the poet, the walker, the student
and lover of all primitive open-air things."

PLACE

In these photographs, the subject or place dominates the image, superseding all other visual elements. Place can also be the imaginative use of depth to create the illusion of a three-dimensional scene on a two-dimensional page.

Falls on Stony Creek varnish autumn leaves,
Catskill Mountains Park and Preserve

Long shadows on ice, Willowemoc Creek,
Catskill Mountains Park and Preserve

Hillside graced with large-flowered trillium, Chenango County

"*The river never seems so much a thing of life as in the spring when it first slips off its icy fetters. The dead comes to life before one's very eyes. The rigid, pallid river is resurrected in a twinkling. . . .*

Columbine and ferns thrive beside rushing water,
Watkins Glen State Park

Ice buildup along Lake Ontario's shore, Tibbets Point Lighthouse

. . . You look out of your window one moment, and there is
that great, white, motionless expanse; you look again, and
there in its place is the tender, dimpling, sparkling water."

Bluebells adorn the forest floor, Finger Lakes National Forest

*Waves whipped up by high winds pound Cayuga Lake's shore,
Finger Lakes*

*Overleaf: Surf-pounded cliffs along the Atlantic Ocean,
Montauk Point, Long Island*

"
  *. . . and in a moment more I stepped from the woods and stood
upon the shore of the lake. . . . There it was at last, sparkling in
the . . . sun and as beautiful as a dream. . . ."

Field of blooming lilies, Allegany State Park

Snow-covered cornfield and barn, Jefferson County

"*He who marvels at the beauty of the world in summer will find equal cause for wonder and admiration in winter. It is true the pomp and the pageantry are swept away, but the essential elements remain — the day and the night, the mountain and the valley, the elemental play and succession and the perpetual presence of the infinite sky.*"

Golden mist at sunrise over Lake Durant,
Adirondack Park and Preserve

Water drips from maple, Whey Pond, Adirondack Mountains

"*Just at the point where the sun is going to rise,*
and some minutes in advance of his coming, there
sometimes rises straight upward a rosy column;
it is like a shaft of deeply dyed vapor, blending with and
yet partly separated from the clouds, and the base of which
presently comes to glow like the sun itself."

Spring runoff in Chittenango Creek, Madison County

Falls on Sanders Kill, Shawangunk Mountains

Overleaf: Golden light accentuates Heart Lake
and the High Peaks region, Adirondack Park and Preserve

"Now [the stream] comes silently along on the top of the
rock, spread out and flowing . . . then drawn into a narrow
canal only four or five feet wide, through which it shoots,
black and rigid, to be presently caught in a deep basin with
shelving, overhanging rocks, . . ."

Maple leaves decorate rock fence,
Catskill Mountains Park and Preserve

Emerging cattails in Bowman Lake, Bowman Lake State Park

"
. . . and there was a rill of water, the beginning of the
creek that wound through the valley below; . . .

Nature's eternal cycle, Adirondack Park and Preserve

*Snow envelops the west branch of the Ausable River,
Adirondack Park and Preserve*

*. . . farther on, in a deep depression, lay the remains of an
old snowbank; . . .*

Meandering trail winds through trillium,
Selkirk Shores State Park

Wintry morning at Mongaup Pond,
Catskill Mountains Park and Preserve

Overleaf: Rock outcrop, Hudson River

. . . Winter had made his last stand here, and April flowers
were springing up almost amid his very bones. . . ."

SOFT LIGHT

Light is the most important aspect of the visual world. The quality of light is affected by the presence or absence of atmospheric conditions such as water vapor, dust particles or smoke. When the sun's harsh rays are subdued by high overcast or light fog, deep shadows fill with soft, diffused light. Textures and sharp edges are smoothed; colors become saturated. The contrast between highlight and shadow is compressed, creating ideal conditions for photographing close- to medium-range images.

Wooden dory at dusk, Long Island

Glassy waters flow over varnished rock, Finger Lakes

The sky's glossy reflection in a pool of sugar maple leaves,
Adirondack Park and Preserve

"*The time of the falling of leaves has come again. Once
more in our morning walk we tread upon carpets of gold
and crimson, of brown and bronze, woven by the winds or
the rains out of these delicate textures while we slept. . . .*

Red maple suspended over Whey Pond,
Adirondack Park and Preserve

Apple trees and leafless hillside,
Catskill Mountains Park and Preserve

Overleaf: Abundance of trillium enhances the forested shoreline,
Cayuga Lake

. . . How beautifully the leaves grow old! How full of light
and color are their last days! . . ."

Spring flourishes along Pixley Falls, Pixley Falls State Park

Chittenango Falls, Chittenango Falls State Park

"A *small river or stream flowing by one's door has many attractions. . . . One can make a companion of it; he can walk with it and sit with it, . . .*

Flowering dogwood brightens a bare forest near East Hampton,
Long Island

Water flows through Watkins Glen, Watkins Glen State Park

. . . or lounge on its banks and feel that it is all his own. It
becomes something private and special to him. . . .

American Falls on the Niagara River, Niagara Falls

Black Dome and Blackhead Mountain,
Catskill Mountains Park and Preserve

Overleaf: Middle Falls on the Genesee River,
Letchworth State Park

. . . You cannot have the same kind of attachment and
sympathy with a great river; it does not flow through your
affections like a lesser stream."

Columbine clings to cliffs, Hudson River

Ice formations on Plattekill Creek,
Catskill Mountains Park and Preserve

"*In wild, delicate beauty we have . . . the columbine, for*
instance, jetting out of a seam in a gray ledge of rock, its
many crimson and flame-colored flowers shaking in the
breeze; . . ."

Maple leaves and granite boulders, Marcy Brook,
Adirondack Park and Preserve

Cascading Bash Bish Falls, Taconic State Park

"*The rocks have a history; gray and weatherworn, they
are veterans of many battles; they have most of them
marched in the ranks of vast stone brigades during the ice
age; they have been torn from the hills, recruited from the
mountaintops, . . .*

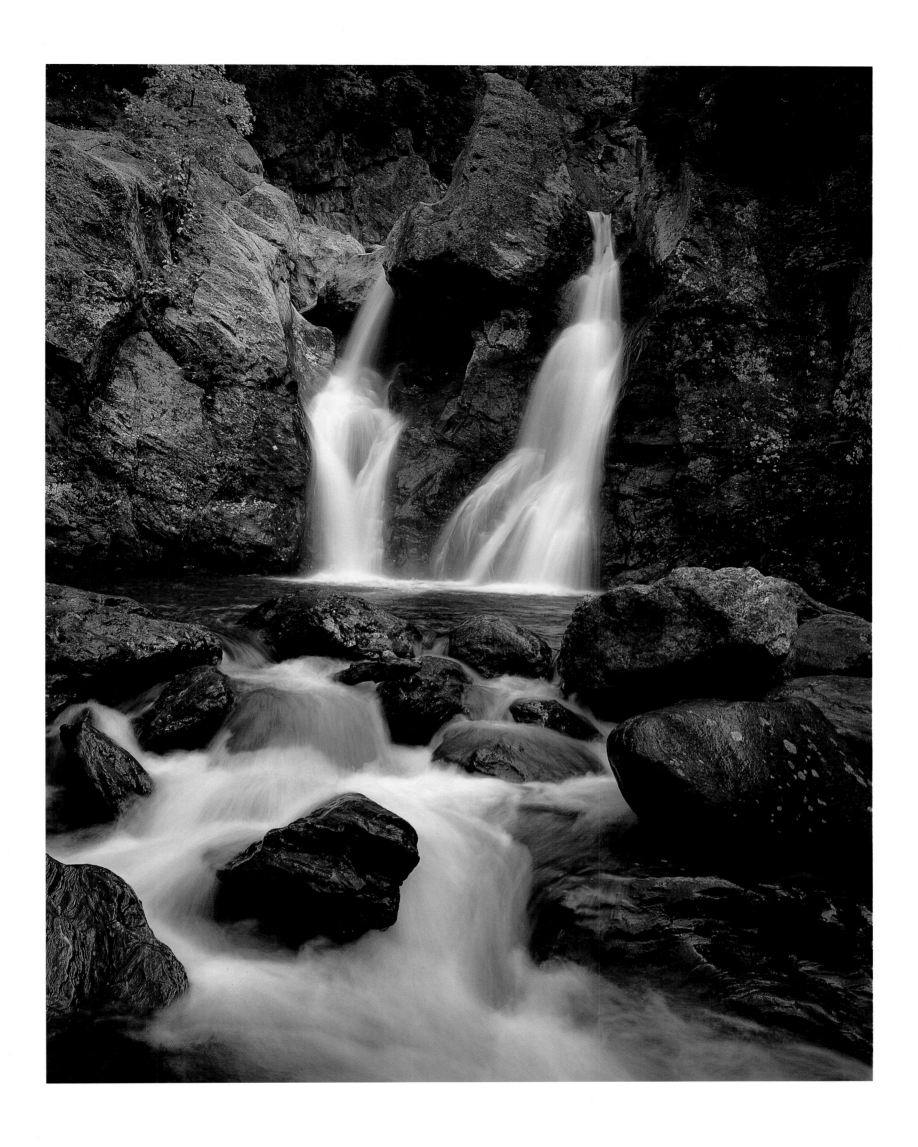

Wooden dory in placid waters, Long Island

Surf motion at Montauk Point Lighthouse, Long Island

Overleaf: Mountain laurel dominates a hillside,
Shawangunk Mountains

. . . and marshaled on the plains and in the valleys; and
now the elemental war is over, there they lie waging a
gentle but incessant warfare with time and slowly, oh, so
slowly, yielding to its attacks!"

MICROCOSM AND MACROCOSM

In photography, microcosm is the intimate, peaceful world below the horizon near one's feet. If compared to music, such an image is soft, subtle and calming.

Macrocosm is the large, the bold, the all-encompassing. Such an image communicates the grandeur and power of a place. It is a climactic, thundering, dramatic piece of music.

Trapps Ridge in the Shawangunk Mountains, Mohonk Preserve

Grass growing alongside wooden dory, Long Island

Clouds reflecting in Oxbow Outlet,
Adirondack Park and Preserve

"*The trees stand so still, the fields are so hushed and
naked, the mountains so exposed and rigid, that the eye
falls upon the blue, sparkling, undulating watercourses
with a peculiar satisfaction. . . .*

Early snowfall covers Millbrook Ridge, Shawangunk Mountains

Virginia creeper, Adirondack Park and Preserve

Overleaf: Autumn leaves suspended on black water,
Adirondack Park and Preserve

. . . By and by the grass and trees will be waving, and the
streams will be shrunken and hidden, and our delight will
not be in them. The still ponds and lakelets will then please
us more."

Barn endures a Keene Valley winter,
Adirondack Park and Preserve

Pink lady's slipper in bloom, Hudson Valley

"
. . . when I go to the woods or fields or ascend to the
hilltop, I do not seem to be gazing upon beauty at all, but to
be breathing it like the air. . . . I am not a spectator of, but a
participator in it. It is not an adornment; its roots strike to
the centre of the earth."

The Genesee River Gorge, Letchworth State Park

*Autumn leaves and foam pattern on Marcy Brook,
Adirondack Park and Preserve*

"
*. . . every drop of water . . . as bright and pure as if the
nymphs had brought it all the way from its source in crystal
goblets, and as cool as if it had been hatched beneath a
glacier.*"

Sunset glow on Atlantic sea scallop shells, Long Island

Wood anemone encompasses beech tree,
Selkirk Shores State Park

Overleaf: Cloud formations over dairy farm,
Catskill Mountains Park and Preserve

"
. . . the bud becomes the leaf or flower; the one is
disentangled from the many and takes definite
form and hue."

Eastern white pine bough covered with fresh snowfall,
Adirondack Park and Preserve

Evening glow on oak leaf, North Lake,
Catskill Mountains Park and Preserve

"*O*ur northern November day itself is like spring water. It
is melted frost, dissolved snow. There is a chill in it and an
exhilaration also. The forenoon is all morning and the
afternoon all evening. The shadows seem to come forth and
to revenge themselves upon the day. The sunlight is
diluted with darkness."

TECHNICAL
INFORMATION

The images within this book were made with either a Tachihara 4x5 field view camera or a Toyo 4x5 field view camera. Lenses of 90mm, 135mm, 180mm, 240mm and 300mm focal lengths were used.

Ektachrome 64 and Fujichrome 50 daylight transparency films were used exclusively.

Exposures were calculated with a Gossen Luna-Pro light meter using both a gray card and values of light in the landscape. Apertures varied from f/5.6 to f/64. Exposures ranged from 1/60 of a second to about 30 seconds.

Snow-covered pines on Trapps Ridge, Shawangunk Mountains